I Can Trick a Tiger

Written by Cynthia Rider,
based on the original characters
created by Roderick Hunt and Alex Brychta
Illustrated by Alex Brychta

OXFORD
UNIVERSITY PRESS

Floppy was dreaming.
He was in the jungle.

A tiger jumped out.
"Got you!" he said.

"I can trick a tiger,"
said Floppy.

"Look out!" said Floppy.

"There is a bee on your nose."

"Oh no!" said the tiger,
and he let Floppy go.

A crocodile jumped out.
"Got you!" she said.

"I can trick a crocodile,"
said Floppy.

"Look out!" said Floppy.

"There is a bee on your nose."

"Oh no!" said the crocodile,
and she let Floppy go.

A snake slid out.

"Got you!" she said.

"I can trick a snake,"
said Floppy.

"Look out!" said Floppy.
"There is a bee on your nose."

"Oh no!" said the snake,
and she let Floppy go.

A rabbit jumped out.

"Got you!" said Floppy.

"Look out!" said the rabbit.
"There is a bee on your nose."

Buzzzzzzzz!

"Oh no!" said Floppy.

Talk about the story

Why did the tiger let Floppy go?

What would you do if you had a bee on your nose?

How do you think Floppy felt when the bee landed on his nose?

Have you ever played a trick on anybody? Was it a funny trick?

Rhyming words

Match the things that rhyme.